Contents

Crimes & Punishment	55
-Judgment Day-	
(Am I on Trial?)	
Maaaaaaaaaaaaaaaate!	59
It's Your Destiny	60
All Politicians Are Arseholes	63
Fluidic Space	66
Heathen Man	67
CrEaTiViTy	69
Rejection	71
Fake News	73
Cruel & Unusual Punishment	75
Anonymous	77
Brave New World	79
Nudity	82
What is Love?	85
Do We Need Leaders?	88
Ying & Yang	89
Don't Be Normal	91
Big Brother	93
FUCK!	96
Desire	99
The Idiot	100
Unrequited Love	102
Rock'n'Roll	104

Where Did You Meet?

Where did you meet?
The CENTRE of the UNIVERSE!

The black hole?
The epicentre of EXCITEMENT!
The focus of culture!
The cross-roads of imagination!

Glebe Library?
The bull's-eye of action!
The Pineal Gland of pleasure!
The G-spot of desire!

Your apartment?
The clitoris of orgasms!
The nucleus of existence!
The parliament of decision making!

Somewhere on Greek St?
The kitchen of nutrition!
The High Street of materialism!
The Stock Exchange of Capitalism!

Kings Court?
The seed of creation!

Coles?
The mind of Thought!

Woolworths?
The vastness of Space!
The Halls of Power!
The pussy of Woman!

Bunnings?
The Politburo of Socialism!
The emptiness of Trump's mind!

Oh, ok. Will you be seeing him again?
The lyricism of Bob Dylan!
He wants to!
I said, I'll think about it!
He left crying!
Life can be a BITCH!

Teddy could be your bitch?
I shouted out, as he walked away, head bowed, "We'll meet again, don't know where, don't know when but I know we'll meet again one sunny day!"

Upon hearing those words, he lifted his head, turned it to me & smiled!

To answer your initial question, **The Bagdad Cafe!**

Written by "The Don" & best friend Brian (unbeknownst to him)!
01.04.2020

The End of Days

The end of days are here.
Left is right, right is left.
Confusion rules supreme.
I Can no longer sit in the sun.
I Can longer have any fun.
Complete isolation is the rule.

But it is not the answer.
Power is given freely.
Rules a created daily
Is there an end in sight.
Do I even have any rights....
…..Anymore?

I slink outside, will I be stopped?
Will I be interrogated?
What are you doing?
I'm walking!
You're supposed to be in isolation?
I'm by myself, I reply!
I don't mention my other two,
Myself & I.

For although I am alone,
I am never really alone!
I'm always talking to myself.
Questioning my actions & motives!
"God I'm an IDIOT, I shouldnt've have said that!
I've gone too far!
She won't like me now!
She'll think I'm too needy!"

"I'm going out for some exercise", I say.
I'm lying!
I hate exercise!
"I'm going stir crazy in my apartment!"
I lie again.
I actually love my apartment & it's quite spacious!
"Ok, then!"
The enforcer of "Social Distancing & Isolation" officer, says.

"I'm only going round the block", I say!
"Off you go then!"
"But just this once!"
"You know the rules!"
"Stay at home!"
"No socialising!"
"Forget your old life!"
"This is the New World!"
"Otherwise I'll have to give you a $1,000 fine!"
"It's for your protection & that of others!"
"We are SAVING lives!"
The officer for Social Distancing & Isolation" instructs me!

I lied, again!
I'm actually going to get a coffee, in my trusty old "keep cup" from my local Cafe that is struggling to
makes ends meet.
The Cafe of Perpetual Indulgence!

"The Don"
02.04.2020

A Handmaid's Tale

We watched!
We were horrified!
We asked each other,
"how could they let this happen?"
"Didn't they see it coming?"
"Didn't they see the signs?"

It's not that straight forward!
It's not that clear!
Situations change rapidly!
Fear is everywhere!

We must close our borders!
We must stay indoors!
Isolation is the answer!
Please close your doors!

Don't talk to strangers!
Don't touch any one at all!
In fact we suggest to sterilise your hands,
Wear a face mask for even more protection!

There is no mention of human intimacy,
No mention of hugs,
No mention of making love!
Only of "Social Distancing" rule of 1.5 metres.
I wander how that works when you sleep with someone?

Do not stop.
Do not linger.
Do not socialise.
Do not cough.
Do not sneeze.
Do not breathe.

We are a "Social Disease"!

Walk in a bubble!
Please, don't make any trouble!
Do as you are told!
Do not think!
Do not act!

Do not pray.
God had closed his door too!

"We're all in this together!"
Together in isolation is not together!

The streets are almost empty!
Warning signs flash their message of "Social Distancing & Isolation"!
"Stay at home!"

Lockdown is the new norm.
Locked in.
Locked up.
A prisoner in your own home.

No more freedom.
No more fun.
No more happiness.
No more friendships
A life of solitude.

Guards are at supermarket doors!
Security guards look scary!
Don't look at them,
That's acknowledging their power & authority!

I try to remain calm.
I try to stick to my routines.
I try to remain positive.
I try to see the light at the end of the tunnel!

I hug someone, anyone that will let me!
I think I'm a rebel!
I'm breaking the rules!
I'm an anarchist!
I ask for a kiss, is that going to far?
I ask for a fuck.
I've done it now!

She says "sure".
I get excited.
"$250 cash for one hour, full service".
I'm shattered!
I thought she liked me.
"I've only got $100 on me", I say
"Keep saving", she coolly replies.

I'm back in isolation!
One of my own doing this time!
I have no friends anymore!
Only imaginary one's!
I placate myself!
It's better than going psycho!
We are all alone anyway!
I rationalise!

"Even the President of The United States must sometime have to stand naked!"

A Handmaid's Tale

"The Dan"
02-04-2020

All Alone in My Lighthouse Tower

There is no way outta here,
Said the loner to his shadow.
No confusion here,
I need no relief.
Business men are going down
Unemployed eating dirt.
Everyone alone in the line,
Hasn't any value or worth.

Gotta have a reason,
The loner didn't speak,
There are many here,
Who think that life is no joke!
But I am not one of those!
So let us talk falsely now.
The time is getting close!

All Alone in my Lighthouse Tower
I never kept a view!
I never came & went
I didn't think I needed too.
Inside in darkness,
The emptiness began to die.
No riders were approaching,
No wind, no sounds, no cry.

"The Don", 03.04.2020

What Is Freedom Anyway?

Be careful what you touch.
Be careful what you do.
Be careful who see.
Be careful what you say.

There are dolphins in the river
There are goats on our streets.
There is less pollution.
Ever since humans have been off there feet.

Everyone is ZOOMING!
Everyone is having a great time.
Everyone is happy.
Every is having fun!

No more noises on the streets!
No more cars either.
No more hooligans roaming at night
No more crime as well.

Stay at home!
Be safe!
We're here for you!
If you ever need any help?

Maybe, this is the way it should be?
Maybe, I've been wrong?
Maybe, life is better this way.
Maybe, we will all get along!

I know I'm crazy.
People tell me ALL the time.
I never seem to know when to stop.
I never seem to listen!

I always seem to cross the line.
I always seem to put my foot in it.
I'm the one with the loudest voice.
But nobody wants to listen.

I've learnt to live within myself.
To take the sticks & stones.
To ride the ebbs & flows.
The roundabouts & narrow streams.

This is my FREEDOM!
To let it ALL go by!
To ride on my own white horse.
Like they did so long, long ago!

"The Don"
05.04.2020

I Read the News Today

(All quotes taken from "The Sunday Herald-NSW", newspaper headlines, 05.04.2020)

"Virus vigilantes are dobbing in neighbours accused of breaching the rules."

"Terrible choice looms even if curve flattens."

"Is the social curse worse than the disease?"

"While we are forced to stay 1.5 metres apart, in some ways we have never been closer together".

"If one person's allowed to sit in the park, everyone's gonna want to sit in the park".

"Strange days indeed: how to stay sane when the world stops turning."

"We must know when limits on liberty end."

·Don't deny students their social lives."

"Life isn't fair. Keep calm & carry on."

"Little sympathy for 'suffering' isolated celebs."

·Just add you: water, sun & soil are waiting to save your sanity."

"So pollies can drop ideology & fix things? Never let them forget it!"

"Now I'm like, I wouldn't want to be in lockdown with anyone but you".

"We want justice!"

"Pubs to become morgues."

"Room for joy to still blossom."

"Party online."

"Secret life of 90 year-olds."

"Home alone."

"Why cash is no longer King."

"The Don"
05.04.2020

Power is a Disease!

Power is good!
Who doesn't want it?
Everyone wants it!
It makes you feel strong.
It makes you feel alive.

I've seen it in action.
The effect it can have.
It changes you from within.
Insidious as Hell.
It happened to me.

You may have good intentions.
Be pure of heart & mind.
Be gentle & kind.
Be father or a mother.
It doesn't take sides.

People around treat you differently.
You are important & stand tall.
They respect & even admire you.
Eager to help & please.
But some will hate & mistrust you.

I am no longer like you.
I have Power to wield.
Like Thor's mighty hammer.
I can make you & break you.
And FEAR is my weapon that unleash.

I can ask you to move on if I want to.
But, if you show me some lip or disrespect.
I can fine you very quickly.
I can make you feel like you are nothing at all.
Just like a rag or a soccer ball.
A plaything for me to kick around, just for some fun.

Power is a Disease!
Of that I am sure!
It is the act of allowing someone to tell you what to do.
To allow them to control you & make decisions on your behalf.
And this is where the problem lies!
In this simple act of letting someone else speak for me,
And I lose my INDIVIDUALITY!

Power is a Disease!

"The Don"
05.04.2020

Listen To the Experts

Listen to the experts,
Hear what they have to say.
They know everything.
We must what they tell us,
Or we will all pay.

They are the best in their fields!
Their knowledge is immense!
We must listen to the experts,
And put our lives into their hands.

They should tell us what to do.
Tell what to eat.
Where we can go out during the day,
Or stay inside & sleep.

They should make ALL the decisions for us,
For it is true they know it ALL.
Their no way we can argue against them,
They have a Doctorate & maybe more.

So, why do I feel so uncomfortable?
Why do I feel I have to resist.
"Resistance is futile"!
They insist, insist, INSIST!

I feel this growing rebellion inside me,
I don't want to be tied down.
I don't want to stay inside,
I want to roam around!

I don't want to listen to the experts!
It's irrational, I know!
They know EVERYTHING!
And I'm just an IDIOT, for sure!

I don't want to listen to the experts,
What they say & propose just doesn't seem fair,
"Do this, don't do that!"
"We understand these are harsh measures but you'll get used to them....
...... in time!"

We've seen ALL before!
History ALWAYS repeats!
I've said it ALL before!
Lockdown rules, lockout laws,
Stay in, stay out,

Don't listen to the experts,
They never get it right!
They might have ALL the knowledge
But they certainly don't have any INSIGHT!

They don't understand her humanity!
They don't understand freedom!
They don't understand that knowledge has to be tempered with feelings.
The head & the heart are one!

A being is not a play thing.
Whatever it may be!
It is a living create with the right to be!
To exist without proving anything.
To live & to let be.

So don't listen to to the experts!
Hahahahaha,
Just listen to me!

"The Don"
06.04.2020

Crazy Times

These are crazy times you hear people say!
It's never been like this before.
Things were different then, a long time ago.

The whole world is going crazy!
The whole world is going mad!
When are we going to be normal?
The way things used to be?

The world has ALWAYS been crazy!
This is nothing new!
There has always been chaos.
This is very true.

In the 1990s it was the fall of the Soviet Union!
In the 1980s it was the Chernobyl Nuclear Power Plant accident!
In the 1960s it was "The Flower Power" revolution.
In the 1950s it was the Atomic Age!

In the 1940s it was World War 2!
In the 1920s it was The Great Depression!
In the 1900s it was WW1 & The Spanish Flu!

History books are littered with crazy times!
This is nothing new!
So let us not think it strange!
We've been through it ALL before!

The world has ALWAYS been crazy!
That is very TRUE!
We are nothing special, different or new!
The world has ALWAYS been crazy!

"The Don"
06.04.2020

Online Socialising

Stay connected,
Make new friends,
Reconnect to old ones,
Learn a new skill,
Try something new.
You can do all of this.
With "Online Socialising"!.

Why not try "ZOOMING",
It's stock market shares are booming!
There's yoga & meditation,
Painting & creating.
Even Pornhub is in on the action.
One month free with "Online Socialising"!

You won't even know you're all alone.
Stuck in you little prison dome.
It's a cubicle for sure,
With just a window & a door!
But way more than that, with "Online Socialising"!

It's a portal into new worlds,
Of fantasy & escape!
To make you forget about your existence,
That you're just a prisoner in a box,
If it wasn't for "Online Socialising"!

I Love "Online Socialising",
I feel sooooooooooooo connected!
I have so many friends now,
More than I ever expected!
I have learnt so many new things with "Online Socialising".

I don't ever want to go back to the way things were before.
To the prehistoric days of dinosaurs.
To the time of human contact,
That was so messy & impure.
In the "REAL" world before, "Online Socialising"!

I feel soooooooooooo connected,
The world is at my finger tips.
Order my food & have it delivered to my door,
With no human interaction!
This is sooooooooooooo much more FUN, with "Online Socialising".

I don't want to go back!
I don't want this to ever end.
To live here forever,
In social isolation.
This is the world I want now, the world of "Online Socialising"!

"The Don"
07.04.2020

I'm Insane!

You're Crazy.
You're weird.
You're mad.
You're a loony bin.
You're insane!

There must be something wrong with you.
You need help.
You're strange.
Just grow up!
You're insane!

Just grow up.
Act you're age.
Now you're just being silly.
You're gross.
You're insane!

Nobody acts like you.
You never take anything seriously!
You have a foul mouth.
You say "FUCK" a lot.
You're insane!

You're a psycho.
You're a lunatic.
You just don't know when to stop.
You always cross the line.
You're insane!

You talk too load.
You never listen.
You talk too much.
You laugh too load
You're insane!

You make no sense.
You talk shit.
You speak nonsense!
You talk rubbish.
You're insane!

You're full of shit.
You're full of crap.
You love the sound of your own voice.
You're up yourself .
You're insane!

You never clean the house.
You never wash the sheets.
You never put the dirty dishes in the dishwasher.
You never clean the toilet.
You're insane!

You live like a princess.
Expect others to do things for you.
You live like a "KONG".
You're delusional.
You're insane!

Wake up to yourself.
Take things seriously!
Life is not a joke or a comedy!
For God's sake stop acting like a child.
You're insane!

You're lazy, you just stay in bed.
What the fuck do you do anyway?
What did you get up to today?
"Nothing much. Just the same old!"
You're fucked in the head & you're insane!

I swear you are regressing!
It's not cute or endearing.
It's not charming or sexy.
It's just pathetic.
Because I swear you're INSANE!

"The Don"
07.04.2020

Too Kind

Stop licking my arse.
Stop feeding my ego.
Tell me the truth.
Stop being too kind!

Is it any good?
Is too personal?
Are you just saying that?
Stop being too kind!

I need to you to tell it to me straight.
You have problems with connection!
Stop sucking up to me.
Stop being too kind!

Am I too direct?
How does it sound?
Do you think it's any good!
Stop being too kind!

I think it's excellent!
I think it's very impressive!
Is it too much?
Stop being too kind!

It's all good!
Be serious!
Stop pushing my ego & tell me the truth!
Stop being too kind!

I am being serious!
Did you even read it?
Of course I FUCKING read it!
Stop being too kind!

Never mind!
Hey don't get angry!
It is NOT too personal!
Stop being too kind!

It provides clear information about your skills.
It is very detailed!
It is full & complete.
Stop being too kind!

I hope it's gonna work.
Stay POSITIVE!
Everything will work out in the END!
Stop being too kind!

"The Don"
08.04.2020

There Is Nothing!

There is no certainty.
There is no future.
There is no past.
There is no tomorrow.
There is no yesterday.
There is nothing!

There are no atoms.
There are no stars.
There no matter,
There is no sky.
There is no land.
There is nothing!

There is no Heaven.
There is no Hell.
There is no God.
There is no Devil.
There is no sin.
There is nothing!

There is no Life.
There is no Death.
There is no Light.
There is no meaning.
There is no meaningless.
There is nothing!

There is no Good.
There is no Bad.
There is no Right.
There is no Wrong.
There are no morals.
There is nothing!

There is no Left.
There is no Right.
There is no Middle.
There is no Politics.
There are no Ethics.
There is nothing!

There is no Creation.
There is no Evolution.
There is no Science.
There is no Philosophy.
There is no Thought.
There is nothing!

There is no pleasure.
There is no pain.
There is no suffering.
There is no path.
There is no road.
There is nothing!

There is no struggle.
There is no angst.
There is no crisis.
There is no chaos.
There is no order.
There is nothing!

There is no plan.
There is no map.
There is destiny.
There is no fate.
There is chance.
There is nothing!

There is nothing.
Nothing there is.
It cannot be understood.
It cannot be imagined
It cannot be defined.
There is nothing!

Nothing exists.
It is pure.
It is indescribable.
It is unfathomable.
It blows your mind.
There IS nothing!

Nothing exists.
Let go of the "Something".
Accept the Nothingness of all.
The Freedom that this brings.
Nothing left to cling onto.
There is nothing after all!

"The Don"
10.04.2020

Fugitives On the Run

Like a band on the run.
We're gonna have some fun!
My mum & I are fugitives on the run.
And I don't even have a gun!

Being chased by the Law!
Criminals who want more!

More freedom.
More space.
More happiness.
More nature.
We're fugitives on the run.
We're gonna have some fun!

No more self isolation.
No more incarceration.
No more incubation.
No more frustration.
We're fugitives on the run.
We're gonna have some fun!

No more anti socialisation.
No more procrastination.
No more hibernation.
We are for LIBERATION!
We're fugitives on the run.
We're gonna have some fun!

We're gonna out run the Law.
We're gonna bust down the door.
We're gonna make a run for it.
And we're not scared a bit.
'Cause we're fugitives on the run.
We're gonna have some fun!

The great open road is our destination.
We're running the gauntlet for some rest & recreation.
If we're caught by the Law for our indiscretion.
I'll tell the truth & say she's my relation.
We're fugitives on the run.
We're gonna have some fun!

Like Bonnie & Clyde of old.
Like Ma Baker & her kin so bold.
Like Paul McCartney's "Band on the Run".
We're a Mother & a son.
We're fugitives on the run.
We're gonna have some fun!

Yes, we're gonna make a run for it.
Escaping this crazy nightmare for a bit.
My mum is eighty-eight years young & fighting fit.
We're gonna be fugitives on the run.
We're gonna have some fun!
We're fugitives on the run!
And I don't even have a gun!
Oh noooooooooooooooooo!

"The Don"
09.04.2020

Fear

Fear is everywhere.
Fear is insidious.
Fear is debilitating.
Fear is in the air.

You see Fear.
You can taste Fear.
You can smell Fear.
You can hear Fear.

Fear immobilises.
Fear paralyses.
Fear terrorises.
Fear dehumanises.

Fear is created.
Fear is generated.
Fear is promoted.
Fear is rewarded.

Fear of failure.
Fear of rejection.
Fear of loneliness.
Fear of sickness.

Fear of poverty.
Fear of robbery.
Fear of loss.
Fear of Death.

"You give me fear (You give me fear) when you kiss me."
"Fear when you hold me tight (you give me fear)."
"Fear in the mornin'."
"Fear all through the night."

"Everybody's got the fear."
"That is somethin' you all know."
"Fear, isn't such a new thing."
"Fear, started long time ago."

"Thou givest fear, when we kisseth."
"Fear, with thy flaming youth."
"Fear, I'm on fire."
"Fear, yea I burn forsooth!

"He gives me fear, with his kisses"
"Fear, when he holds me tight"
You give me fear.
She gives me fear.
He gives me fear.
They give me fear.
It gives me fear.

Fear!
Fear!
Fear!
Fear!

"The Don"
10.04.2020

Crucifixion Day

Happy Crucifixion Day!
It's such a happy day!
It's the day we all get saved.
At least that's what they say!

Yes, I have been a Sinner!
Yes, I have sinned!
Yes, I have broken The Ten Commandments!
Yes, I have been bad & naughty!

Yes, have pursued Desire!
Yes, I have pursued Pleasure!
Yes, I have sought to to seek The Treasure.
Yes, I have delved into The Fire!

Yes, I have been guilty of Pride.
Yes, I have been guilty of showing Envy
Yes, I have been guilty of showing Gluttony.
Yes, I have been guilty of showing Greed.

Yes, I have been guilty of showing Lust.
Yes, I have been guilty of showing Sloth.
Yes, I have been guilty of showing Wrath.
Yes, I have been guilty of all "The Se7en Deadly Sins".

But I rejoice in my sinful ways!
I dance to the music of Sin.
For I know that I am a Sinner Man!
I have no mask to hide behind!

The life of a Sinner Man is honest!
There are no lies to conceal.
I do not have to pretend to be someone else.
Because I'll tell you straight, I am a Sinner Man!

I am a Sinner Man, I'll say it in your face!
I'll look into your eyes & say yes, I'm a Sinner!
I've been a Sinner all my life.
I wouldn't have it any other way!

I life of lies & pretence.
Of hiding who you really are.
Of social niceties, accolades & advancements.
Is not a life I seek or desire!

Yes, I am a Sinner Man!
This day is a day of celebration!
The day on which ALL Sinners can proudly come out & say:
"Yes, I am a Sinner & I wouldn't have it any other way!"

"Oh, Sinner Man, where ya gonna run to?"
"Oh, Sinner Man, where ya gonna run to?"
"Oh, Sinner Man, where ya gonna run to?"
All on that day, Crucifixion Day?

"Oh, Sinner Man, where you gonna run?"
"Oh, Sinner Man, where you gonna run?"
"Oh, Sinner Man, where you gonna run?"
All on that day, Crucifixion Day?

Yes it's, Crucifixion Day!
Yes it's, Crucifixion Day!
Yes it's, Crucifixion Day!
Crucifixion Day!

Crucifixion Day!
Crucifixion Day!
Crucifixion Day!
Yes it's, Crucifixion Day!

"The Don"
10.04.2020

Resurrection Day

Arise from your sloth.
Arise from your slumber.
Arise from your sleep
Arise from your dream.

Arise from your bed.
Arise from your couch.
Arise from your online.
Arise from your television.

Arise from your monitor.
Arise from your floor.
Arise from your chair
Arise from your iPhone.

Arise from your throne.
Arise from your cellar.
Arise from your dungeon.
Arise from your prayers.

Arise from your isolation.
Arise from your desolation.
Arise from your incarceration.
Arise from your decapitation

Arise from your humiliation.
Arise from your masturbation.
Arise from your fornication.
Arise from your extermination.

Arise from your expatriation.
Arise from your annihilation.
Arise from your atomisation.
Arise from your sublimation.

Arise from your procrastination.
Arise from your subjugation.
Arise from your suffocation.
Arise from your disqualification.

Arise from your objection.
Arise from your obliviation.
Arise from your obligation.
Arise from your dehumanisation.

Arise from your rationalisation.
Arise from your intellectualisation!
Arise from your proselytisation.
Arise from your sterilisation.

Resurrection Day is here.
It's time to go to the pub.
It's time to drink a beer.
Resurrection Day is here.

Arise, arise, Resurrection Day is here.
Arise from your DEATH.
A new Dawn has arisen.
Arise, arise, Resurrection Day is here.

"The Don"
10.05.2020

Men Think With Their Cocks!

Why is Love so difficult?
Why is Love so hard?
To maintain relationships?
To maintain friendships?
Because Men Think With Their Cocks!

The World is FUCKED today!
But it's always been FUCKED!
Today's World is no different!
The people in power are the same, men!
And Men Think With Their Cocks!

Women understand about Love.
They know that it's not about sex.
They Know that Love is food for the heart!
And not just a quick Fuck!
Because Men Think With Their Cocks!

Men do not understand Love!
They think it's "Wam, Bang, Thank You Man!"
A quick FUCK is all that's needed!
No respect, no kindness, no compassion.
Because Men Think With Their Cocks!

From the young boys & men that make up "Isis" in the Middle East.
"Kim Jong-un" the Supreme Leader of North Korea.
"Donald Trump" President of The USA.
"Vladimir Putin" the Russian President.
They are ALL Men who Think With Their Cocks!

LOVE is in your being!
LOVE is in your Heart!
LOVE is in your Soul!
LOVE is who you Are!
Men Think With Their Cocks!

LO♥E is in Life!
LO♥E is in thinking!
LO♥E is in your actions!
LO♥E is in everything you do!
Men Think With Their Cocks!

When you LO♥E there is nothing else to be!
When you LO♥E there is nothing else you can do!
When you LO♥E there there is no choice!
When you LO♥E there everything is very clear!
Men Think With Their Cocks!

Men do not understand this!
It's cultural that's true!
But that is no longer an excuse!
It cannot be used as a justification for men's HORRENDOUS actions.
Men Think With Their Cocks!

Men have to be taught what is Lo♥e!
Men have to be taught how to Lo♥e!
Men have to STOP thinking with their cocks!
Men, it's time to move out of the way!
And let Women rule with their HEARTS!

"The Don"
12.04.2020

The Ballad of "The Outlaw Don"

Not many fugitives take their mums along these days.
That's because he's bad, real bad.
He's the meanest, baddest outlaw in the land.
But he loves his mum.
He's "The Outlaw Don".

He's an outlaw.
He's on the run
He's with his mum.
He's was sitting on his bum.
He's "The Outlaw Don".

The "Pigs", that's "cops" for ye younger folk.
Gave a mighty chase.
But they were no match for "The Donmobile".
It was brown & shaped like a turd.
But it flew like bird by "The Outlaw Don".

He put the pedal to the metal of "The Donmobile".
With the "Pigs" in pursuit.
They tried stop you at a road block.
Roadblock? What roadblock?
"The Outlaw Don" in "The Donmobile" eat roadblocks for snacks!

They scattered the road with tyre spikes to try & stop him.
But little did they know that "The Donmobile" used tyre spikes as toothpicks!
Did his mum enjoy being on the run?
She was having a ripping time!
With her son, "The Outlaw Don".

The "fuzz", that's "cops" for ye younger folk.
Were chasing him for hours.
There must've been at least 10 cops, all with their sirens blaring.
Finally, that mighty "Donmobile" broke down.
That hero to so many children, "The Outlaw Don" was caught!

He was asked to get out with his hands in the air.
He shouted his innocence!
"I'm with my mum!"
"And I don't even have a gun!".
But the cops were cruel & mean to "The Outlaw Don".

They told him to "Spread them".
Then they frisked, strip searched & violated him!
Little did they know that he was enjoying this.
"Oh Lucky me!", he shouted.
He was a pleasure seeker, our hero, "The Outlaw Don".

"I have to tell you that I've got a lotta shit in there!"
He tried to warn the cop with the glove on her hand.
And sure enough, that's what they found!
He didn't know where else to hide his stash of drugs but up his arse!
"You're nicked", they said to our hero, "The Outlaw Don".

"Ok, you've caught me!" he said to the cops.
"But before you take me away, can I say goodbye to my dear ol' mum & give her one last hug & kiss?"
"Where is your mum?", asked a burly cop with a huge gut hanging over his belt.
"She's in the backseat of "The Donmobile", replied "The Outlaw Don".
So, he woke his dear old mum, gave her a kiss, a hug & said his last goodbye, our hero, "The Outlaw Don".

Now, the moral of this story, is to always look after your mum.
Take her out for a drive now & then.
Even if you're on the run.
Because most mums will still love you, no matter what you've done.
And that's the story of our hero, "The Outlaw Don".

Yeah, that's "The Ballad of "The Don"!

"The Don"
14.04.2020

Clarity

Clarity of Thought.
Clarity of Purpose.
Clarity of View.
Clarity of Direction.
Clarity of Form.
Clarity of Aim.
Clarity of Destiny.
Clarity of Reason.
Clarity of Feeling.
Clarity of Truth.
Clarity of Intuition.
Clarity of Sight.
Clarity of Being.
Clarity of Ideals.
Clarity of Ideas
Clarity of Conscience.
Clarity of Action.
Clarity of Absurdity.
Clarity of Chaos.
Clarity of Meaning.
Clarity of Meaninglessness.
Clarity of Nothingness.
Clarity of Mind.
Clarity of Mindlessness.
Clarity of Faith.
Clarity of Faithlessness.
Clarity of Past.
Clarity of Future.
Clarity of Moment.
Clarity of Consciousness!
Clarity of Heart.
Clarity of Love.
Clarity of LIFE.
Clarity of DEATH.

"The Don"
15.04.2020

My Friend Brian

He's got the heart of a lion.
He's the body of a panther.
He's go the mind of scholar.
That's my friend Brian.

He's meek & mild.
Never tries too hard.
He likes to stay in the shadows.
That's my friend Brian.

He's wit is razor shape.
He never seems to grow old.
Although, he can't grow a beard.
That's my friend Brian.

I met him in year 7 of high school in 1972.
At Drummoyne Boys' High, when we were just 12 years old.
And we've been friends ever since.
That's my friend Brian.

He's a student of knowledge.
He's an intellectual.
He likes a good argument.
That's my friend Brian.

He likes to eat very slowly,
He likes to chew his food!
Nothing too fast for him.
That's my friend Brian.

He loves his cricket.
I've never understood.
It must be an Aussie thing?
That's my friend Brian.

He also loves his footy.
That's Rugby League, my friend.
The game they play in Heaven.
That's my friend Brian.

He had a bit of tumble recently,
His ticker wasn't working right.
They had to operate all day & night!
That's my friend Brian.

He was told that this was it!
He wouldn't make it through.
But they didn't know that he is a fighter.
That's my friend Brian.

Even though we met so many years ago.
And had many adventures along the way.
Friendships like ours never die.
We'll always be best buddies!
That's my friend Brian.

We are both old now.
The old school doesn't exist anymore.
It's become Scalabrini Village.
An old people's home.
Maybe that's where I'll end up.
With my friend Brian.

"The Don"
16.04.2020

Ode to the Greatest Game of All

Now, some of you might like golf.
Some of you might like tennis.
There are others who will like boxing.
Then there are those who say they like cricket.
But, there is only one game that fires me up.
And it's the game they play in Heaven.
And that's the great game of Rugby League.
Some say, of which I'm one,
That it's The Greatest Game of ALL.

Some of you might like wrestling,
Others might like basketball.
Then there those who like baseball.
There is only one game that's got it all.
Poetry & brutality in equal measure.
It is both complex & yet so simple.
A dance, a ballet in motion.
An opera that could have been written by Mozart.
That's what makes it The Greatest Game of ALL..

It beautiful & graceful to watch when the big men fly.
Their hits are like a 10 tonne truck has hit ya.
But they are quickly back on their feet, because these are no ordinary men.
They are super heroes to both little children & oldies alike.
They embody the ANZAC spirit at Gallipoli, so long ago!
When, against all odds, they fought a useless battle on a distance shore!
Yes, they lost that battle but that's not the point.
It is the bravery of those men that we remember them for.
This is the same bravery & courage, that makes it The Greatest Game of ALL.

It's true it can be boring & predictable at times.
But this is only those that are not aficionados of the game.
For it's not just a bash fest of brutality, blood & gore, which it is.
It is also a game of strategy, skill & attrition, of wearing you opposition into the ground!
It's a game of relentless energy, of explosive power & force!
That will leave you gasping for air from the excitement of the clash.
The two men in the middle, yes it needs two, have no clue about the rules.
The video ref also gets it wrong, even though it's in slowmo.
But, we all go home happy, because we've seen The Greatest Game of ALL.

"It's long enough, it's high enough & it's straight between the posts".
The great Frank Hyde used to say after every try.
When the great Graham Langlands & Billy Smith would but on their magic for "The Mighty Dragons".
There was was the dazzling "Shnoz Sterlo", Peter Sterling, dancing his way through missed tackles.
Who could forget prop, "The Brick With Eyes", Glenn Lazarus, who had another life as a forgettable politician.
Unforgettable players of a bygone era who not were great exponents of the great game but had personality plus, such as:
Steve "Blocker" Roach, "The Beaver", Steve Menzies, who could play & sleep at the same time. What a gift!
Wayne "Junior" Pearce, "Ok Tedi", Adrian Lam, Noel "Crusher" Cleal.
All legends of The Greatest Game of ALL.

Who can forget Cliff "Cliffy" Lyons, who played until he was forty, drinking & smoking during every game? A legend!
They don't make players like him any more!
A rare breed of player!
What talent!
What skill!
What personality!
A real favourite with the kids & a great role model!
There was "The Chief", Paul Harragon who had no regard for his body in the first ten minutes of a game.
"The Wombat", Graham Eddie who didn't like to tackle.
All immorals of The Greatest Game of ALL.

"Spud Carroll", Mark Carroll, "Fatty", Paul Vaughn & many, many more who make up the pantheon of great players.
And Let's not forget players of "The Modern Era" of the game such as:
Andrew "Joey" Johns, Darren "Lovechild" Lochyer, Johnathan "JT" Thurston, "Billy the Kid" Billy Slater & Cameron "Cam" Smith (the dirtiest player to ever take to the field & 36 years young, still playing today).
Their time may have long gone.
But they will always live on, in our hearts & memories.
For they were great warriors, some might even call them Gods.
And I am happy to call myself one!
We shall never forget them!
Let's raise a beer & say hip, hip hooray, to all those...
That all played, The Greatest Game of ALL.

The great game of Rugby League!

"The Don"
17.04.2020

Everything's Fake!

Fake food.
Fake leather.
Fake looks.
Fake hair.
Fake breasts.
Fake butt.
Fake eyes.
Everything's Fake!

Fake songs.
Fake music.
Fake truth.
Fake beliefs.
Fake myths
Fake schools.
Fake news.
Everything's Fake!

When you stop & look around you,
Nothing is real.
Nothing is genuine.
Everything's Fake!

Fake humor.
Fake ideas.
Fake religions.
Fake relationships.
Fake Love.
Fake happiness.
Fake friendships.
Everything's Fake!

Fake air.
Fake politicians.
Fake leaders.
Fake countries.
Fake ideals.
Fake justice.
Fake morality.
Everything's Fake!

I can't believe it.
It can't be true!
No, not even you.
Everything's Fake!

Fake stories.
Fake history.
Fake winners.
Fake trends.
Fake laws.
Fake rules.
Fake system.
Everything's Fake!

Fake art.
Fake science.
Fake plants.
Fake cities.
Fake sex.
Fake humans.
Fake life.
Everything's Fake!

"The Don"
17.04.2020

Illusion or Reality?

Am I real?
Are you real?
Is this just an illusion?
What is Reality?
Is Everything just an Illusion or Reality?

Are we in a Matrix?
Are we in a Multiverse?
Are we just a dream?
Pinch yourself to see!
Is Everything just an Illusion or Reality?

Are you Alive?
Can you really Feel?
Are we just Zombies?
From "The Walking Dead"!
Is Everything just an Illusion or Reality?

Am just dreaming?
Are you just dreaming?
If this is a dream?
Then it's a bloody NIGHTMARE!
Is Everything just an Illusion or Reality?

"I'll let you be in my dream, if I can be in your dream?"
That was Bob Dylan's dream.
I am a "Daydream Believer"!
That was "The Monkeys" dream.
Is Everything just an Illusion or Reality?

"Dream Weaver".
That was Gary Wright's dream!
"I had a dream!"
That was Martin Luther King's dream.
Is Everything just an Illusion or Reality?

When you stop & think about.
It drives your mind insane.
It can even blow your tiny mind.
When you ask the question.
Is Everything just an Illusion or Reality?

It can make you go crazy!
It can make you go numb!
It can paralyze you with Fear.
It can scare you shitless.
Is Everything just an Illusion or Reality?

Am I all alone?
Do I really exist?
Do you really exist?
I am I a dream dreaming about you?
Is Everything just an Illusion or Reality?

Does God exist?
Does Lo♥e exist?
Is there a Heaven?
Is there a Hell?
Is Everything just an Illusion or Reality?

Ashes to ashes, dust to dust.
In this cosmic, quantum ether.
The Space-Time continuum is a mystery!
It is an eternal enigma!
Is Everything just an Illusion or Reality?

"The Don"
19.04.2020

Where Has All the Humour Gone?

Do you remember the "Jackie Gleason Show"?
How about "Gilligan's Island"?
Or the funniest spy of all, "Get Smart"?
Who can forget the amazing "Monty Python Show"?
So I have to ask,
Where Has All the Humour Gone?

That funny man, Jerry Lewis, alone or with partner Dean Martin.
The zany, Mel Brooke's, who made "The Producers" & "Men in Tights"!
He provocatively & famously said that, everything could & should be made fun of.
Even "The Holocaust!"
Where Has All the Humour Gone?

Even "The Holocaust", should be made fun of.
Comedy should not be censored!
Even to be offensive!
Of course he was condemned from pilar to post for his views.
Where Has All the Humour Gone?

The difference between comedy & tragedy is very small.
It depends on where your standing & the position of it all.
See someone walking into a tree, is a comedy!
You walking into a tree a tragedy!
Where Has All the Humour Gone?

Who didn't laugh at the shenanigans of Colonel Hogan, Commandant Klink &
Sargeant Shultz in "Hogan's Heroes"?
The hilarious comedy show about nothing, "Seinfeld".
With those misfits, Jerry, Elaine, George & Kramer.
Where Has All the Humour Gone?

Of course, two of my favourite comedians were Abbott & Costello.
As a child I loved watching their movies!
I lo♥e slapstick comedy!
"Who's on First?", "Naturally"!
Where Has All the Humour Gone?

It has stood the test of time!
And this is what makes good comedy.
It is non-epocal.
It is funny regardless of when it was made or where.
Where Has All the Humour Gone?

"The Don"
19.04.2020

Rainy Night Bob (Years 1960- 2020) -Fragments of Bob Dylan

(All are lines that I remember from Bob Dylan songs)

*(These are all fragments of lyrics from songs directly from my memory.
I have not checked them against the original, even though I was tempted too.
So, I suspect there will be a lot of errors with the original but that's what memory does.
It introduces errors, for better or worse.)*

"Yes, and how many years can the cannonballs fly before they're forever banned?
Yes, and how many years can some people exist before there allowed to be free?
Yes, and how many times can a man turn his head pretending he just doesn't see?
Yes, and how many ears must one man have before he hears people's cries?"

"You've got a lotta nerve, to say you are my friend!
When I was down, you just stood there laughing!
You say I let you down but you know it was not like that!"

"Take me disappearing through the smoke rings of my mind.
Through the foggy ruins of time.
Far past the frozen leaves.
The haunted, frightened trees.
Out to the windy beach.
Far from the twisted reach of crazy sorrow.
Yes, to dance beneath the diamond sky.
With one hand waving free.
Silhouetted by the sea.
Circled by the circus sands.
With all memory & fate.
Driven deep beneath the waves.
Let me forget about today until tomorrow."

"And I hope that you die.
And that your death will come soon.
And I'll watch them carry you casket,
In the pale afternoon.
And I'll watch till you're lowered, down to your deathbed.
And I'll stand over your grave, to make sure that your dead!"

"Like the water they runs down your drain."

"Even the President of The United States must sometime have to stand naked!"

"It's all right ma, I'm only bleeding!"

"God said to Abraham "kill me a son".
Abe said "man you must be having me on?"
"Where do you want this killing done?"
God said "out on Highway 61!""

"They're selling postcards of the hanging.
The painting the passports brown."

"The sandman draws circles.
Up & down the block."

"Someone's got it in for me, who it is, I can only guess."

"You're an Idiot babe. I wonder how you still know how to breathe."

"Something is happening here but you don't know what it is, do you? Mr Jones!"

"I'm walking through streets that are dead.
I'm talking to you in my head.
I am so tired, my head is so wired.
I'm sick of Lo♥e!
I'm so over it.
I'm sick of Lo♥e!
I'm Lo♥e Sick!"

"There must be someway outta here?
Said the Joker to the Thief.
Too much confusion here.
I can't get no relief.
Business men they drink my wine.
Plowmen dig my earth.
None of them along the line.
Know whatever it is worth."

"The moral of this story, the moral of this song, is that one should never be,
where one does not belong!"

"Now all the criminals in their suits & their ties are free to drink martinis & watch the sun rise.
While Reuben sits like Buddha in a ten foot cell. An innocent man in a living hell!"

"Broken dreams.
Broken schemes.
Broken promises.
Everything's broken!"

"Sundown, yellow moon.
I replay the past.
I know every scene by heart.
It all by so fast.
If she's passing back this way
I'm not that hard to find,
Tell her she can look me up,
If she's got the time."

"Either I'm too sensitive, or else I'm getting soft!"

"Frankie Lee & Judas Priest, they were the best of friends."

"Where have you been my blue eyed son?
Where have you been my darling young one?
What did you see my blue eyed son?
What did you see my darling young one?
What did you hear my blue eyed son?
What did you hear my darling young one?
It's a hard.
It's a hard.
It's a hard.
It's a hard.
It's a hard rain, a-gonna fall!"

"It's a slow, slow train coming.
Coming round the bend."

"'Twas was in another life,
One of toil & blood.
When darkness was virtue.
And the road was full of mud.
She came up to me so gracefully,
And took my crown of thorns.
Come in she said I'll give you,
Shelter from the storm."

"Now, in a hilltop village,
They gambled for my clothes.
I pleaded up my salvation.
But they gave me a lethal dose
I offered up my innocence.
And got repaid with scorn.
Come in she said I'll give you,
Shelter from the storm."

"What was it you wanted?"

"I wish, I wish in vain.
If we could be that way again!
A thousand dollars at the drop of a hat.
I'd give it all gladly,
If we could be again like that."

"Lo♥e is just a four letter word."

"I'm not gonna work for Maggie's Ma no more.
I'm not gonna work for Maggie's Pa no more.
I'm not gonna work for Maggie's brother no more.
I'm not gonna work for Maggie's sister no more.
No, I'm not gonna work for Maggie's farm no more."

"You're gonna have to serve somebody.
Well, it could be the Devil or it could be the Lord.
But, you're gonna have to serve somebody!"

*"And you who philosophise disgrace.
And criticise all fears.
Wipe the smile away from your face.
Now's the time for your tears!"*

*"They'll stone you when you're at the breakfast table.
They'll stone you if you're young & able.
They'll stone you & then they'll say, "Get Fucked!".
Well, I would not feel so all alone.
Everybody must get stoned!"*

*(With thanks to Robert Zimmerman.
Your words have been an enormous part of the fabric of my life for over fifty years, from my early teens.)*

*"The Don"
19.04.2020*

CRIMES & PUNISHMENT
-JUDGMENT DAY-

(Am I on trial?)

Who made you the judge & jury?
What is it that I've done?
Why all the questions?
Am I on trial?

What am I guilty of?
Have I been accused by others?
Has there been a judgment?
Am I on trial?

I didn't know I'd committed a crime?
I didn't know I'd done something wrong?
Have I been sentenced?
Am I on trial?

The jury has decided!
The verdict has arrived.
I've been found guilty!
Am I on trial?

I didn't know there was a trail?
I wasn't given a chance to testify!
To put my side of the story!
Am I on trial?

I plead my innocence!
I plead my ignorance!
I plead insanity!
Am I on trial?

Am I on trial here?
What is my crime?
What are the charges?
Am I on trial?

The crime is "Murder One"!
A crime most despicable & foul!
Murder of your innocence.
Am I on trial?

Murder of your sanity!
Murder of your Love!
Murder of your humanity!
Am I on trial?

You're crimes are so heinous.
They are are unimaginable in cruelty.
So full of hatred & vengeance.
Am I on trial?

You have been found guilty!
By the highest court in the land!
Guilty for your actions!
Am I on trial?

Guilty your Honour!
You are guilty for your crimes!
You'll have to do your time!
Am I on trial?

You will be punished severely.
Your punishment will be harsh.
You will have to suffer greatly.
Am I on trial?

You are sentenced to Life in prison!
A Life long sentence of suffering.
A life long sentence of misery.
Am I on trial?

Your sentence is to live your life alone!
To wander this barren Earth forever
Without any friends, family or home.
Am I on trial?

"Here comes "The Judge!"

"Here comes "The Judge!"

No, there was no trial.
No chance to plead your case!
No chance to plead your innocence!
Your are guilty nevertheless!

There are no appeals.
This decision is final.
You've been found GUILTY!
GUILTY! GUILTY! GUILTY!

"How does it feel?
How does it feel?
To be on your own.
With no direction home.
Like a complete unknown."

I do not recognise this court!
I do not have to prove myself to you
I do not have to prove myself anyone.
I am NOT on trial!

I do not need you to validate me!
I do not seek or need your approval.
I do not need accept your judgment.
I am NOT on trial!

Case dismissed!

"The Don"
20.04.2020

Maaaaaaaaaaaaate!

Mate!

MAATE!

MAAATE!

MAAAAATE!

MAAAAAAATE!

MaaaaAAAAAAAAATE!

MaaaaaaaAAAAAAAAAAAAAaaaaaaTE!

MaaaaaaaaaAAAAAaaaaaaaAAAAAATE!

MAAAAAAAAAAAAAAAAAAAAAAAaaaaaaTE!

MAAAATE!

MaaaaAAAAAAAATE!

MAAAAAAAATE!

MAAAAAAAAAAAAAAaaaaaaaTE!

Mate!

MAte!

MAte!

Mate!

Maaate!

Maaaaaate!

For my "Mate", Sonny!

"The Don"
20.04.2020

It's Your DESTINY!

You & me.
It's meant to be.
Living in Harmony.
Can't you see?
It's your Destiny!

You & me.
It's meant to be.
You can run,
But you can't hide from me.
Because, it's your DESTINY!

Hee, hee, hee.

You & me.
It's DESTINY!
It's meant to be!
Can't you see!

You can run.
But you can't hide from me.
It was meant to be!
Can't you see!

Hee, hee, hee.

Just like a tree.
In history.
It's simplicity.
It's multiplicity.

Hee, hee, hee.

It's so Lovely,
It's humanity.
It's probability.
You can't escape your DESTINY.

Hee, hee, hee.

You must agree.
It's meant to be.
You & me
It's your DESTINY!

Hee, hee, hee.

It's simplicity.
You've gotta agree?
It's our sexuality.
It's your DESTINY!

Si, si, si.

In harmony.
We will be.
Forever for eternity!
It's your DESTINY!

Si, si, si.

From obscurity.
To clarity.
There's nothing more to see.
It's your DESTINY!

Si, si, si.

It's a profanity.
Not to be.
Can't you see.
It's your DESTINY!

Si, si, si.

It's integrity.
For you to be with me.
It's meant to be!
It's your DESTINY!

You cannot disagree.
It was meant to be.
You & me.
It's your DESTINY!

It's serendipity.
You must agree.
You & me.
It was meant to be.
It's your DESTINY!

You & me.
It's harmony.
It's meant to be.
Can't you see?.
Because it's DESTINY!

You & me.
It's meant to be.
Living in Harmony.
Can't you see?
It's your Destiny!

It's your DESTINY!
It's your DESTINY!
It's your DESTINY!
It's your DESTINY!

Livin' in Harmony!
It's your DESTINY!
Livin' in Harmony!
It's your DESTINY!

"The Don"
21.04.2020

ALL POLITICIANS ARE ARSEHOLES

No, this can't be true?
There was JFK, Paul Keating & Bob "Hawkie" Hawke.
Just to name a few!
And what about Jucinta Ardurn or Barack Obama?
The first African-American President of The United States of America.
They were pretty good you might say?
But I continue to stand firm.
All politicians are ARSEHOLES!

History is littered with them
From Alexander the Great, to Cleopatra.
Julius Caesar, Hammurabi, Henry XIII.
And who could forget the most notorious one of all?
Whose name we still shudder at the thought of.
The name we fear to mention.
The Devil incarnate himself, Adolf Hitler.
The greatest ARSEHOLE politician of them all!

He murdered 6 million.
In the gas chambers they died.
Men, women & children.
Very few survived.
His reason was to exterminate.
To purify his race he claimed.
All politicians are ARSEHOLES!

Their profession is to liar.
They are the very best at that.
They will lie straight faced at you.
They will not flinch, blink or bat an eye.
They will lie straight at your face.
All politicians are ARSEHOLES!

They are fake.
They are frauds.
They are deceitful.
They are immortal.
They are unethical.
All politicians are ARSEHOLES!

They seek power.
They seek sex.
They seek money.
They seek need to satisfy selfish appetites
They seek need to satisfy selfish pleasures.
All politicians are ARSEHOLES!

They are cunning with their deceit & lies.
They will dazzle you with sweet promises.
They will ask you to trust them.
They will tell you that they know your needs.
They will convince you that they are working for the greater good.
All politicians are ARSEHOLES!

They are slick.
They are persistent.
They are insidious.
They do not give in.
They will keep on saying that they are doing this for you

Don't fall for their cheap parlor tricks.
Of smoke screens & mirrors!
Scratch the surface & you will see the truth.
They is nothing there, underneath.
They are hollow men!
All politicians are ARSEHOLES!

They are empty suits walking around.
They carry hollow men inside.
They have no substance!
The suits are filled with hot air.
The stench of lies & broken promises.
All politicians are ARSEHOLES!

Let us remove their suits.
Let them stand naked.
Let them be seen for what they really are.
Old men with old ideas that have died long ago.
What is standing there in front of you is DEATH itself.
All politicians are ARSEHOLES!

But we NEED politicians, I hear you say!
Who's gonna run the Government?
Who's gonna lead the way.
But just stop & think about it,
If they were doing such a good job.
We wouldn't be thinking this way!

We wouldn't be disillusioned & pissed off with them.
We wouldn't be in decay.
The fact of the matter we don't need them
No matter what they say!
They are the ones that need us!
We are their source of power.

So, let's get rid of them once & for all.
It better this way.
We can make decisions for ourselves.
We can govern our own way.
It's only then that we'll have a true Democracy.
One where people have the power & no one else is in the way!

"The Don"
20.04.2020

Fluidic Space

It's mobility.
It's transparency.
It's clarity.
It's fluidity.
It's Fluidic Space.

It's got permubility.
It's got frequency.
It's got malubility.
It's got ductility.
It's Fluidic Space.

It's a mentality.
It's a capacity.
It's a creativity.
It's a philosophy.
It's Fluidic Space.

It's a Spirituality.
It's a religiousity.
It's an unbelievability.
It's a curiosity.
It's Fluidic Space.

It's the space between spaces.
It's the space inside your Mind.
It's the space inside Dark Matter.
It's the space on Space-Time.
It's Fluidic Space.

It's the space inside White Matter.
It's the space inside Anti-Matter
It's the space inside your Head.
It's Fluidic Space.

It's the space inside a Black Hole.
It's the space inside a Worm Hole.
It's the space inside a Space Portal.
It's the space between The Multiverse.
It's Fluidic Space.

It's the space inside the Universe!
It's the space inside Nothingness
It's the space inside Somethingness.
It's the space inside my Soul.
It's Fluidic Space.

It's tranquility.
It's reciprocity.
It's sexuality.
It's community.
It's Fluidic Space.

It's communality.
It's informality.
It's non-conformity.
It's surreality.
It's Fluidic Space.

It's integrity.
It's ingenuity.
It's familiarity.
It's universality.
It's Fluidic Space.

"The Don"
23.04.2020

HEATHEN MAN

I'm dirty.
I'm naughty.
I've got a foul mouth.
I've got a filthy mind.
I'm a Heathen Man.

I'm rude.
I'm crude.
I'm crazy.
I'm lazy.
I'm a Heathen Man.

I'm loud.
I'm profane.
I'm sacrilegious.
I'm blasphemous.
I'm a Heathen Man.

I'm a comedian.
I'm a humanitarian.
I'm a libertarian.
I'm a Gregorian.
I'm a Heathen Man.

I'm anti-social.
I'm a hypocrite.
I'm a lie.
I'm fake.
I'm a Heathen Man.

I'm sexual.
I'm bisexual.
I'm homosexual.
I'm transsexual.
I'm a Heathen Man.

I'm non-religious.
I'm anti-spiritual.
I'm the Anti-Christ.
I'm the Devil's Child.
I'm a Heathen Man.

I'm an anarchist.
I'm a socialist.
I'm a capitalist.
I'm a unilateralist.
I'm a Heathen Man.

I'm a Loser.
I'm Rasputin.
I'm Casanova.
I'm Don Juan.
I'm a Heathen Man.

I'm a lion.
I'm a tiger.
I'm a panther.
I'm an animal.
I'm a Heathen Man.

I'm powerful.
I'm irresistible.
I'm manipulative.
I'm beautiful.
I'm a Heathen Man.

I'm a trouble maker.
I'm a deal breaker.
I'm controversial.
I'm a mystery.
I'm a Heathen Man.

I'm enigmatic.
I'm argumentative.
I'm competitive.
I'm illusive.
I'm a Heathen Man.

I'm a Sinner Man
I'm a Hollow Man.
I'm a Wicker Man.
I'm a Danger Man
I'm a Heathen Man.

"The Don"
23.04.2020

CrEaTiViTy

It's what we do.
We can't help it.
That's what Life is.
It's about CrEaTiViTy!

But I'm not creative.
I hear people say.
I can't draw, write or make music.
I have no, CrEaTiViTy!

That's what they say.

CrEaTiViTy is inside us.
CrEaTiViTy is in our Hearts
CrEaTiViTy is in our soul.
We are CrEaTiViTy!

CrEaTiViTy is in our very Being.
CrEaTiViTy is in our very Seeing.
CrEaTiViTy is in our way of Thinking.
Living is CrEaTiViTy.

CrEaTiViTy is Energy.
CrEaTiViTy is Sensory.
CrEaTiViTy is Imagination.
We have no choice in CrEaTiViTy!

CrEaTiViTy is an Explosive power.
CrEaTiViTy is takes you to Higher power.
CrEaTiViTy is mind expanding.
There is Nothing without CrEaTiViTy!

CrEaTiViTy just your blows your mind!
CrEaTiViTy is an ever expanding Universe.
CrEaTiViTy is infinity.
There is power in CrEaTiViTy!

But I have no CrEaTiViTy.

I hear people say. Just BELIEVE in yourself.
Believe in your CrEaTiViTy!

It doesn't matter to what you do.
What is important is that it comes from YOU.
It's your own self-expression.
No one else has your CrEaTiViTy!

CrEaTiViTy is yours & yours alone.
CrEaTiViTy only has value to you.
CrEaTiViTy is who you are.
I Love my CrEaTiViTy!

CrEaTiViTy is my way of Life.
CrEaTiViTy is my nourishment.
CrEaTiViTy is my Spiritual Path.
DEATH is Life without CrEaTiViTy!

Death of the Soul is no CrEaTiViTy.
Death of the Heart is no CrEaTiViTy.
Death of the Mind is no CrEaTiViTy.
Death of Humanity is no CrEaTiViTy!

CrEaTiViTy is Passion.
CrEaTiViTy is Ecstasy.
CrEaTiViTy is Sexuality.
Love is CrEaTiViTy!

CrEaTiViTy is Light!
CrEaTiViTy is Fire!
CrEaTiViTy is Beauty!
There is only, CrEaTiViTy!

Don't be a walking zombie.
Be a Being of CrEaTiViTy!
CrEaTiViTy it's the way to BE!
CrEaTiViTy!

"The Don"
24.04.2020

Rejection

Rejection, a stab in the Heart.
Rejection, hurts from the start.
Rejection, hits you like a train.
Rejection, happens again & again.

Rejection, a kick in your gut.
Rejection, a boot up your butt.
Rejection, a poke in your eye.
Rejection, makes you wanna die.

Rejection, it hurts like Hell.
Rejection, it tolls the Bell.
Rejection, it's painful to see.
Rejection, it's always been here.

Rejection, is everywhere.
Rejection, it's even in the air.
Rejection, it's a living thing.
Rejection, it's The King.

Rejection, run away!
Rejection, run & pray.
Rejection, run & hide.
Rejection, it'll take you for a ride.

Rejection, it'll catch up to you.
Rejection, it'll do what it has to.
Rejection, it'll tear you apart.
Rejection, it'll destroy your Heart.

Rejection, bring it on.
Rejection, your my song.
Rejection, I have no fear.
Rejection, it's so clear.

Rejection, I laugh in your face.
Rejection, there is no race.
Rejection, you have no power over me.
Rejection, I am free!

Rejection, you have lost the game
Rejection, I am not the same.
Rejection, I warm your embrace.
Rejection, you have lost the race.

Rejection, I Lo♥e you now.
Rejection, there is no more sorrow on my brow.
Rejection, you make me happy.
Rejection, no more making me feel crappy.

Rejection, I call your name.
Rejection, you're not the same.
Rejection, you're my friend.
Rejection, this is the end.

Rejection.
Rejection.
Rejection.
Rejection.

Come to me!
Come to me!
Come to me!
Come to me!

Chiamami!
Appelle-moi!
¡Llámame!
Ruf mich an!

"The Don"
25.04.2020

FAKE NEWS

Fake news is everywhere.
Journalism has gone down the drain.
Push your point of view.
It doesn't matter if it isn't true.
Why stick to the facts.
Just write whatever you fucking like.
The media is owned by a few anyway.
They just want to push their point of view.

Rupert Murdoch owns a lot.
He owns "Fox Media".
Did you know that he was born in Australia.
Before he became a dual citizen.
He's an American now.
Married to Jerry Hall, one of Mick Jagger's many ex's.

Murdoch likes to own politicians in Australia.
Through his company "News Corp".
He likes to own one particular politician.
The Prime Minister of Australia!
Whoever he happens to be.
Yes, it's a "He", he doesn't like women as leaders.
Maybe it's because they won't play his game.
And see him for what he is, an ARSEHOLE!

He owns "The Telegraph" in NSW, & other newspapers across Australia.
It is especially dishonest, conservative & opinion driven.
It NEVER let's the facts get in the way of spreading is vile diatribe of SHIT.
Through this mouthpiece he spreads his Fake News.

He destroyed Kevin "Kevin07" Rudd.
He annihilated Julia Gillard, our first & only female Prime Minister.
He owned Tony Abbott, who was an idiot any way.
He brought down Malcolm Turnbull, who "couldn't be owned"!
According to Malcolm himself, so there is no corroborating evidence to back this up.
And of course, we we know that politicians don't lie!
Especially, Malcolm TurnBull!

If you don't get the answer you want?
Don't worry, just print whatever you like.
Just make it up.

If the evidence is not there to support your argument or point of view.
Don't worry, just print whatever you like.
Just make it up.

If the situation is not to your liking.
Don't worry, just print whatever you like.
Just make it up.

Don't say once!
Say it over & over & over again.
Remember, if you say a lie long enough it becomes REAL!

You might even come to believe it yourself.
If you're lucky!
That way you might be able to sleep enough.
Although, you probably say that there is plenty of time to sleep....
......when you're DEAD!

"The Don"
25.04.2020

Cruel & Unusual Punishment

We are prisoners in our own homes.
We have not committed any crime.
Put we're doing the time.
It's Cruel & Unusual Punishment.

We have been forced to live in "iso".
We have been told it's for our own good.
We have been told it's for the benefit of all.
But it's Cruel & Unusual Punishment.

We can go out for exercise that's.
Don't stop, don't loiter, don't congregate.
Don't engage in any social intercourse.
Such, Cruel & Unusual Punishment.

You can do alone or pairs, that's all.
Make sure you observe "Social Distancing".
1.5m apart, that's the LAW.
Such, Cruel & Unusual Punishment.

We've been stuck inside since I don't know when.
In fact, I've come to think that it's NEVER gonna end.
It could be another six months or more, I hear them say.
Such fucking, Cruel & Unusual Punishment.

"What doesn't kill us, makes us stronger", the saying goes.
"Survival of the fittest", is the Darwinian way.
Let's rebel & go outside.
Staying inside, is such, Cruel & Unusual Punishment.

Let us reclaim the streets.
Let us reclaim touching each other.
Let us reclaim our Lives.
Let's escape from this most, Cruel & Unusual Punishment.

Let us hug each other once more.
Let us kiss each other without any FEAR.
Let us make Lo♥e, like we're meant to.
Let us break this Cruel & Unusual Punishment.

FOREVER & NEVER again!

"The Don"
27.04 2020

Anonymous

I am invisible.
I am nobody.
I am nothing.
I am unknown.
I am nameless.
I am unnamed
I am nowhere.
I am transparent.
I am enigmatic.
I am mysterious.
I am immaterial.
I am emptiness.
I am nebulous.
I am misty.
I am inconsequential.
I am valueless
I am worthless.
I am unremarkable.
I am blank.
I am clear.
I am clarity.
I am ethereal
I am air.
I am unseen.

I am unsighted.
I am formless.
I am shapeless.
I am Anti-Matter.
I am unimaginable.
I am unidentifiable.
I am unidentified.
I am traceless.
I am unfathomable.
I am surreal.
I am illusive.
I am cosmic.
I am meaningless.
I am faceless.
I am Alien.
I am unreal.
I am anyone.
I am no-one.
I don't exist.
I am wanted.
I am Dangerous.
I am ANONYMOUS!

"The Don"
28.04.2020

Brave New World

I'm having trouble sleeping at night.
I'm overthinking everything.
I'm got a bad feeling in my gut.
Is this a Brave New World?

Freedoms easily lost.
Don't stand still.
Don't sit down.
Is this a Brave New World?

"There is something going on here but you don't know what it is?
Do you, Mr Jones?"
Bob Dylan screams in 1965.
Is this a Brave New World?

Conspiracy theories are everywhere.
It's "Agenda 31".
My friend Zac proclaims.
Is this a Brave New World?

"What's in those huge buildings?"
"They have no windows!"
"With massive electric cabling!"
Is this a Brave New World?

Paranoia is everywhere.
Fear runs deep.
Did I tell you I can't sleep?
Is this a Brave New World?

Given has taken control.
Is this a "State of Emergency"?
Is this "Martial Law"?
Is this a Brave New World?

Download the app?
Your data will be secure.
Big Brother is watching.
Is this a Brave New World?

"I've seen the Future & it's MURDER!"
Prophecies Leonard Cohen.
The Future is here!
Is this a Brave New World?

I have a friend.
She's having trouble sleeping.
She feels something's just ain't right.
Is this a Brave New World?

She's already had a bad experience.
She was stopped at the border.
Police went through her phone.
Without her permission.
"You have no right!"
"I didn't give you permission!"
"You have violated my rights!"
She screamed in protest.
She screamed in disgust
She has a bad feeling in her gut.
She feels something's just not right.
This shouldn't be happening.
Whatever it is, that's happening.
Is this a Brave New World?

I'm feeling scared.
I'm feeling afraid.
"What the fuck is going on here?"
Is this a Brave New World?

I'm getting concerned.
Freedoms easily lost,
Are hard to regain.
Is this a Brave New World?

Freedoms hard fought for,
By brave individuals, such as:
Guy Falkes, Emmeline Pankhurst, Che Guevara, Rosa Parks, Martin Luther King.
Is this a Brave New World?

Don't open your eyes.
I must be sleeping.
This is just a dream I'm in.
Is this a Brave New World?

We were warned in "1984" by George Orwell.
Aldous Huxley wrote about it too.
But nobody bothered to listened or even cared.
Is this the Brave New World?

Helen Garner described it vividly.
"A Handmaid's Tale" was the new future.
"Beware!", she cried, for no one to hear.
It's a Brave New World out there!

"The Don"
29.04.2020

Nudity

Don't be ashamed of your nakedness.
Don't be ashamed of your body.
Don't be ashamed of being naked.
Don't be ashamed of Nudity.

Don't be ashamed of naked body.
Don't be ashamed of your body parts.
Don't be ashamed of being seen naked.
Don't be ashamed of Nudity.

Every man has a cock.
Every woman has a pussy.
We're all part of Nature
Don't be ashamed of Nudity.

Everyone has body hair.
Everyone has breasts.
Everyone is different.
Don't be ashamed of Nudity.

Nudity is natural.
Nudity is organic.
Nudity is normal
Don't be ashamed of Nudity.

We were all born naked.
We will all die naked.
"Even the President of The United States must sometime have to stand naked!"
Don't be ashamed of Nudity.

Don't be bashful.
Don't be shy.
Don't be scared.
Don't be ashamed of Nudity.

Don't fight your body.
Don't be at war with your body.
Don't hated your body.
Don't be ashamed of Nudity.

Lo♥e your body.
Lo♥e yourself.
Lo♥e your naked self.
Don't be ashamed of Nudity.

Stand naked in front of the mirror.
Looked at your naked self.
Lo♥e what you see.
Don't be ashamed of Nudity.

Lo♥e you naked image.
Lo♥e your self deeply.
Even if nobody else will.
Don't be ashamed of Nudity.

Lo♥e your naked body.
Lo♥e it without anything.
Love yourself without your costume on.
Don't be ashamed of Nudity.

Nudity is not bad.
Nudity is not a sin.
Nudity is beautiful.
Don't be ashamed of Nudity.

Lo♥e me for my body.
Lo♥e me for my mind.
Lo♥e me for who I am inside.
Don't be ashamed of Nudity.

You're naked body is your best friend.
It's always with you, right till the very end.
Through thick & thin.
Ups & downs!
Giving both pleasure & pain.
Through the good times & the bad.
It's put up with everything.
It's loyal & non demanding.
Just asking to be cared for.
Lo♥ed & not abused.
What a ride it's been.
So, my sister & brother.
I tell you this from my heart.
Don't be ashamed of Nudity.

Don't be ashamed of Nudity.

Don't be ashamed of Nudity.

Don't be ashamed of Nudity.

Nudity.

Nudity.

Nudity.

"The Don"
30.04.2020

What is Love?

I hear the word "Love" used a lot.
It's not taught at school.
It's not taught at home.
So, What is Love?

We are sent out blind without a road map,
Looking & searching for Love.
We spend our whole lives searching.
So, What is Love?

Sometimes it's a quiet search.
Sometimes it's a loud cry.
A scream of desperation!
So, What is Love?

Love cannot be bought & & sold.
Love is a feeling, that's for sure.
Love is confusing.
Love is complex.
So, What is Love?

There are so many different forms of Love.
There's:
"Tough Love",
"Parental Love",
"Puppy Love",
"Conditional Love",
"Unconditional Love",
"Abusive Love",
"Sexual Love".
"Passionate Love",

"Possessive Love",
"Tormented Love",
"Plutonic Love",
"Romantic Love",
"Sinful Love",
"Casual Love",
"Unrequited Love",
"Jealous Love",
"Self Love",
"Esoteric Love"
"Abstract Love".
"Transcendental Love",
So, What is Love?

Is Love sex?
Can Love hate?
Can Love kill?
Can Love abuse?
So, What is Love?

"I did it because I love you!"
"I loved her or him too much!"
"Love made me do it!"
So, What is Love?

"I lost myself to Love",
"Love is a battlefield",
"Love is a drug",
So, What is Love?

"I love my car",
"I love my cat",
"I love my dog",
So, What is Love?

Can Love be lost & found?
Can you Love too much?
Can you Love too many?
So, What is Love?

"I can only Love one person!"
"I can't Love anymore!"
"What's Love got to do with it?"
So, What is Love?

"I can't Love anymore!"
"I'm all out of Love!"
"The Tunnel of Love"
So, What is Love?

"All you need is Love",
"Whole Lotta Love",
"I'm All Outta Love",
So, What is Love?

"Sunshine of your Love",
"I Want to Know What Love Is",
"Only Love Can Break Your Heart",
So, What is Love?

"Crazy Little Thing Called Love",
"You've Gotta Hide Your Love Away",
"I'll Never Love Again!"
So, What is Love?

Is Love Spiritual?
Can Love be manufactured?
Can Love bleed?
So, What is Love?

"Love is just a four letter word!"

"The Don"
01.05.2020

Do We Need Leaders?

"We need Leaders!"
"We need someone to make decisions!"
"We can't all be Leaders!"
Do We Need Leaders?

"We don't know what to do!"
"Some a born to lead!"
"Others are born to be led!"
Do We Need Leaders?

"We always had Leaders!'
"People want to be led!"
"People can't make decisions for themselves!"
Do We Need Leaders?

"People are basically stupid!"
"People need to be helped!"
"It's not possible for everyone to be Leaders!"
Do We Need Leaders?

"Leaders bring order!"
"Leaders bring a vision!"
"Leaders bring unity!"
Do We Need Leaders?

"Leaders bring strength!"
"Leaders bring social cohesion!"
"Leaders make a society better!"
Do We Need Leaders?

Has there ever been a society without Leaders?
Has there ever been a time when people have not been led?
Has there ever been a time when the "Collective Whole" made the decisions?
Do We Need Leaders?

"I have a dream!"
"Of a time & a world of no Leaders!"
Maybe I'm a dreamer or just crazy?
Do We Need Leaders?

"The Don"
01.05.2020

Ying & Yang

Male & Female.
Love & Hate.
Good & Evil.
Light & Dark
Negative & Positive.
Happiness & Sadness.
Comedy & Tragedy.
Material & Immaterial.
Chaos & Order.
Justice & Injustice
Saints & Sinners.
Moral & Immoral.
Sanity & Insanity.
Life & Death
Ying & Yang.

The concept of "Duality of Opposites".
The "Power of Polar Opposites".
The "Law of Attraction of Opposites".
Although, seemingly opposite in Nature.
Inexplicably, interconnected & interdependent.
Always tethered together for eternity.
But never to meet.
Embraced in this infinite dance.
Swirling through the fabric of Space-Time.
Two Lovers destined to never consummate their Love.

"Dance me to your beauty with a burning violin.
Dance me through the panic till I'm gathered safely in
Lift me like an olive branch and be my homeward dove.
Dance me to the end of love.
Dance me to the end of love."

It's to observe but never participate.
To long but never be longed.
To Love but never be Loved.
To hate but never be hated.
To look but never see.
To listen but never hear.
To speak but never say anything meaningful.
To touch but never feel.
To imagine but never be imaginative.
To live but to never have lived!
To Ying but never Yang.

"The Don"
01.05.2020

Don't Be Normal

You wanna be an individual.
But you're like all the rest.
You wanna be different.
But you're just everyone else.
You wanna be unique.
But so does everyone else.
You wanna dress differently.
But you look like all rest.
You don't wanna conform.
But you do the same same as everyone else.
You wanna be a radical.
But you do the same as the rest.
You wanna be a free spirit.
But you trapped everyone else.
You wanna be a fee thinker.
But you think like all the rest.
You wanna be a Revolutionary.
But you do as everyone else.
You wanna be a rebel.
But you act like all the rest.
You wanna Love.
But you hate like everyone else
You wanna be wanna be an Alien.
But you are like all the rest.
You wanna connect.
But you're disconnected like everyone else
You wanna fly to the skies.
But you're tethered to the ground like all the rest.
You wanna be be free of Fear.
But you're as fearful like everyone else.
You wanna be knowledgeable.
But you're as ignorant as all the rest.

You wanna be selfless.
But you're as selfish as everyone else.
You wanna be kind
But you're as unkind as the rest.
You wanna be happy.
But you are as unhappy as everyone else.
You wanna be innocent.
But you're as guilty as all the rest.
You wanna see.
But you're blind like everyone else.
You wanna hear.
But you're as deaf as all the rest.
You wanna be sexy.
But you're as sexless as everyone else.
You wanna be ageless.
But you're aging like all the rest.
You wanna be an Anarchist.
But you do like all everyone else.
You wanna be Anti-Establishment.
But you live all the rest.
You wanna be Anti-Materialist.
But you buy like everyone else.
You wanna be Real.
But you're as Fake as all the rest.
You wanna be a child forever.
But you're old like everyone else.
You wanna be Alive.
But you're Dead just like all the rest.

I understand!
I don't want to be normal too!
Just like you!

"The Don"
02.05.2020

Big Brother

Big Brother is watching YOU!

Watching everything you DO!
Watching everything you SAY!
Watching everything you PAY!
Watching everything you SEE!
Watching everything you HEAR!
Watching everything you EAT!
Watching everything you BUY!
Watching everything you HIDE!
Watching everything you SMOKE!
Watching everything you DRINK!
Watching everything you LIKE!
Watching everything you HATE!
Watching everything you WATCH!
Watching everything you THEORISE!
Watching everything you HYPOTHESIS!
Watching everything you FUCK!
Big Brother is watching YOU!

Watching everyone you LIKE!
Watching everyone you LOVE!
Watching everyone you MEET!
Watching everyone you GREET!
Watching everyone you RIDE!
Watching everyone you FUCK!
Watching everyone you SUCK!
Watching everyone you FORNICATE!
Watching everyone you HATE!
Watching everyone you ANNIHILATE!
Watching everyone you EXONERATE!
Watching everyone you PUNISH!
Watching everyone you ADMONISH!
Watching everyone you HUMILIATE!

Big Brother is watching YOU!

Watching everywhere you GO!
Watching everywhere you STAY!
Watching everywhere you WORK!
Watching everywhere you PLAY!
Watching everywhere you HIDE!
Watching everywhere you SING!
Watching everywhere you SHELTER!
Watching everywhere you SKELTER!
Watching everywhere you PRAY!
Watching everywhere you LAY!
Watching everywhere you FUCK!
Watching everywhere you PISS!
Watching everywhere you SHIT!
Watching everywhere you FLATULATE!
Watching everywhere you FORNICATE!
Watching everywhere you DIE!

Big Brother is watching YOU!

Watching everytime you are LATE!
Watching everytime you are EARLY!
Watching everytime you are ANGRY!
Watching everytime you are HUNGRY!
Watching everytime you are NAUGHTY!
Watching everytime you are HAUGHTY!
Watching everytime you are CRAZY!
Watching everytime you are LAZY!
Watching everytime you are SEXY!
Watching everytime you are HAZY!
Watching everytime you are FUCKED!
Watching everytime you are DOPED!
Watching everytime you are STONED!

Big Brother is watching YOU!
Big Brother is watching YOU!
Big Brother is watching YOU!
Big Brother is watching YOU!

Watching YOU!

Watching YOU!

Watching YOU!

Watching YOU!

YOU!

YOU!

YOU!

YOU!

"The Don"
02.05.2020

FUCK!

Fuck you!
Fuck me!
Fuck my family!
Fuck my mother!
Fuck my brother!
Fuck everyone!
Fuck work!
Fuck playtime!
Fuck society!
Fuck the Government!
Fuck The System!
Fuck The Establishment!
Fuck Capitalism!
Fuck Communism!
Fuck Fascism!
Fuck Socialism!
Fuck Multinationals!
Fuck Oligarchies!
Fuck Love!
Fuck Hate!
Fuck Narcissism!
Fuck Science
Fuck Religion!
Fuck The Devil!
Fuck God!
Fuck Death!

Just.....

FUCK!

FUCK!

FUCK!

FUCK!

"The Don"
02.05.2020

Celluloid Heroes

(Everyone's a Hero, Everyone's a Star)

Who are your favourite movie stars?
Those actors that will never die.
Because they are immortalised on the Silver Screen.
They will live forever!
Celluloid Heroes never, ever die!

My favourite is the suave, Cary Grant.
Whose real name was Archie Leach.
Who could forget him as the mistaken Roger Thornhill?
In the classic film by Alfred Hitchcock,
"North By Northwest".
What a masterpiece.
Celluloid Heroes live forever!

There was vulnerable & sensitive, Anthony Perkins,
In another Hitchcock classic, "Psycho".
The iconic tough guy, Humphrey Bogart in "The Maltese Falcon" & "Key Largo"
To name but two of his movies.
Celluloid Heroes never, ever die!

But, my all time favourite movie star was Marlon Brando.
A colossus, both on the movie screen & in real life.
There was "The Wild one", "On The Waterfront" & "Apocalypse Now".
And his greatest role of all, "The Don", "Don Vito Corleone in "The Godfather"!
Celluloid Heroes live forever & ever!

Al Pacino as Michael Corleone, in "The Godfather" trilogy!
"I tried to get out but they pulled me back in!"
Robert De Nero in "Taxi Driver".
Jack Nicholson in "One Flew over the Cuckoo's Nest" & "Chinatown".
Paul Newman in "Cool Hand Luke" & "Hud".
And of course the great, Marilyn (Norma Jean) Monroe!
Celluloid Heroes never, ever die!

"I wish my life was non-stop Hollywood movie show.
A fantasy world of celluloid villains and heroes.
Because celluloid heroes never feel any pain.
Celluloid Heroes never really die."

"Oh, celluloid heroes never feel any pain.
Oh, celluloid heroes never really die.
I wish my life was non-stop Hollywood movie show.
A fantasy world of celluloid villains and heroes.
Because celluloid heroes never feel any pain.
Celluloid Heroes never really die!"

"Everybody's a dreamer and everybody's a star
And everybody's in show biz, it doesn't matter who you are."

Everyone's a movie star.
Everyone's a hero.
Everyone is famous.
Everyone's an actor.
Everyone's in a movie.
Celluloid Heroes live forever!

Everybody's a dreamer.
Everybody's a star.
Everybody's in movies.
It doesn't matter who you are.
As we act out our lives in "Life's Long Boulevard"!

Celluloid Heroes never, ever die!

"The Don"
03.05.2020

Desire

Desire has a hold of you.
Desire is telling you what to do.
Desire has you under it's spell.
Desire is a living Hell.

Desire has you by your balls.
Desire has you up against the walls.
Desire will never end.
Desire is not your friend.

Desire will never stop.
Desire will let you drop.
Desire is never satisfied
Desire is not happy until you're crucified.

Desire has no eyes.
Desire just tells you lies
Desire is in your head.
Desire won't let go, until you're DEAD!

Desire!
Desire!
Desire!
Desire!

"The Don"
04.05.2020

The Idiot

I always say the wrong thing.
I always say too much.
I never know when to stop.
I'm The Idiot.

I'm always too loud.
I'm always using the wrong words.
I'm always swearing too much.
I'm The Idiot.

I'm always trying to be funny.
I'm always trying too hard.
I'm try to be the Joker.
I'm The Idiot.

I like to tell a story.
I like to entertain.
I like to make people laugh.
I'm The Idiot.

I like to be rude.
I like to shock.
I like to say "fuck" a lot.
I'm The Idiot.

I like to play with people's minds.
I like to make people think.
I like to create a huge, big stink.
I'm The Idiot.

I like to seem intellectual.
I like to appear intelligent.
I like to be smart.
I'm The Idiot.

I like to appear controversial.
I like to promote controversy.
I like to polemicise.
I'm The Idiot.

I like to be sexy
I like people to like me.
I like to be popular.
I'm The Idiot.

I'm not very successful.
I'm not very smart.
I'm not very sexy.
I'm The Idiot.

I am a loser.
I am a failure.
I am a nobody.
I am The Idiot.

The Idiot

"The Don"
04.05.2020

Unrequited Love

Unrequited Love is the loneliest Love of all!
A Love that is a one way street!
A Love that is not returned.
A Love that is forlorn.
A Love that goes unseen.

Unrequited Love is the loneliest Love of all!
A Love that enchained & enslaves you.
A Love that is always hidden.
A Love that lurks in the shadows
A Love that is never spoken.

Unrequited Love is the loneliest Love of all!
A Love that never speaks.
A Love that is forlorn.
A Love that is hopeless.
A Love that has no home.

Unrequited Love is the loneliest Love of all!
A Love that speaks no words.
A Love that is a longing.
A Love that cannot rest.
A Love that is always alone.

Unrequited Love is the loneliest Love of all!
A Love that cries in silence.
A Love that is full of sadness.
A Love that has gathered cobwebs.
A Love that is not returned

Unrequited Love is the loneliest Love of all!
A Love that has no name.
A Love that lives in darkness.
A Love that lives in vain.
A Love that is never returned

Unrequited Love is the loneliest Love of all!
A Love that sees no light.
A Love that sees no day.
A Love that sees no night.
A Love that is never consummated.

Unrequited Love is the loneliest Love of all!
A Love that everyone's heard of.
A Love that is always empty.
A Love that is full of pain.
A Love that will never bloom.

Unrequited Love is the loneliest Love of all!
A Love that sees always rain.
A Love that is always restless.
A Love that is full of shame.
A Love that will never be set free

Unrequited Love is the loneliest Love of all!
A Love that is a prisoner.
A Love that is locked up.
A Love that shouts in a vacuum.
A Love that will never, ever be heard.

Unrequited Love is the loneliest Love of all!
A Love that never sees the light of day.
A Love that has so much to say
A Love that has no end.
A Love that will never, ever have a friend.

"The Don"
04.05.2020

Rock'n'Roll

Been a long time since we Rock'n'Roll.
Been a long time since we did the stroll.
Ben a long time since you stepped on my blue suede shoes.
Been a long time playing The Blues.

Been a long time since we had a dance.
Been a long time since we made romance
Been a long time since we sang our song.
Been a long & Rock'n'Roll is gone.

Been a long time since I made Love to you.
Been a long time since I Boogied with Stew.
Been a long since I wore my high heeled sneakers.
Been a long time since I saw Tom Petty & The Heartbreakers.

Been a long time since I saw you!
Been a long a I no longer know what to do!
Been a long I've been all alone.
Been a long time without a home.

Been a long time since I've made Love.
Been a long time since I flew like a dove.
Been a long time since I've had fun.
Been a long time sitting with my gun.

Been a long time in the rain.
Been a long time feeling my pain.
Been a long time without a song.
Been a long time & it's a lot of time gone.

Been a long time living in my Head.
Been a long that I wish I was Dead.
Been a long freaking out.
Been a long going out & about!

Been a long time since I Rock'n'Rolled.
Been a long time since I was cajoled.
Been a long time since I was Stoned.
Been a long time since I was boned.

Been a long time since I Rock'n'Rolled.
Been a long time since I did the Stroll.
Been a long since I had a dance.
Been a long time since I made romance.

"It's been a long time, been a long time.
Been a long lonely, lonely, lonely, lonely, lonely time.
Ooh yeah, ooh yeah.
Ooh yeah, ooh yeah.
It's been a long time, been a long time.
Been a long lonely, lonely, lonely, lonely, lonely time."

"Rock'n'Roll, rock, Rock'n'Roll.
Rock'n'Roll, rock, Rock'n'Roll
Rock'n'Roll, rock, Rock'n'Roll
Rock'n'Roll, rock, Rock'n'Roll."

"Hail, hail Rock'n'Roll.
Long live Rock'n'Roll.
Rock, rock Rock'n'Roll."

"Rock'n'Roll ain't noise pollution.
Rock'n'Roll will never die!"

"Let there be Rock".

"Let there be Rock'n'Roll".

"Rock'n'Roll is just, Rock'n'Roll!"

"The Don"
04.05.2020